# THE
# LION
## AND THE SAVANNAH

Text and photographs
**Dave Taylor**

Animals and their Ecosystems Series

A
Bobbie
Kalman
Book

Crabtree Publishing Company

**Animals and Their Ecosystems Series**
Dave Taylor

**Editor-in-Chief**
Bobbie Kalman

**Editors**
Christine Arthurs
Marni Hoogeveen
Janine Schaub

**Design and pasteup**
Adriana Longo

**All photographs by Dave Taylor**

## For Liza

I wish to thank the African Safari Club with whom I traveled while in Kenya. The people of that country have set a standard of wildlife conservation for which the world should be grateful.

Cataloguing in Publication Data

Taylor, J. David, 1948-
    The lion and the savannah

(Animals and their ecosystems)
Includes index.
ISBN 0-86505-364-2 (bound)  ISBN 0-86505-394-4 (pbk.)

1. Lions - Juvenile literature. 2. Lions - Ecology - Juvenile literature. 3. Savannah ecology - Juvenile literature.
I. Title. II. Series.

QL737.C23T3 1990   j599.74'428

350 Fifth Ave.   360 York Road, R.R.4   73 Lime Walk
Suite 3308     Niagara-on-the-Lake   Headington
New York      Ontario, Canada      Oxford OX3 7AD
N.Y. 10118    L0S 1J0           United Kingdom

# Contents

5     **The lion and the savannah**

6     **In search of a new pride**

8     **Strong lion, strong cub**

10     **Life in the pride**

12     **The heart of the pride**

14     **Cute and pampered**

16     **Lion facts**

18     **Life on the savannah**

20     **The grassland grazers**

22     **The predators**

24     **A lion hunt**

26     **What a feast!**

28     **Poachers—the superpredators**

30     **This land is mine!**

32     **Glossary and Index**

# The lion and the savannah

The lion walks slowly through the dried yellow grass. Occasionally he pauses to lift his nose high, sniffing the air to locate the rest of his family group, called a pride. This large male lion is in the prime of life. A furry, black-tipped mane surrounds his face. We shall call him Simba because simba means "lion" in Swahili, the language spoken by many East African tribes. Simba's tale is similar to the story of most African lions.

Simba returns from patrolling his territory. Around him in every direction stretch the grasses of the plain—a vast, flat area of land where few trees grow. Whenever the wind blows, the movement of the grass resembles a billowing sea. A grassland such as this one, which is located in the hot region close to the equator, is called a savannah. People used to travel to this area in eastern Africa to hunt the many large wild animals that live in the savannah ecosystem. Now much of the region is a reserve, a place where the animals are protected. Hunting is no longer allowed, and the animals are free to roam wherever they like. Simba lives in a small part of the reserve where he has set up the boundaries of his domain. Let us follow Simba and his pride through a typical day on the African savannah.

*(opposite) This is Simba, the lion. He stops for a moment to look at a passing herd of elephants.*

*(below) Simba and his pride live on the savannah where great herds of wildebeest and zebra abound.*

# In search of a new pride

At one time Simba lived in a pride made up of his mother, father, brother, sisters, aunts, and uncles. When Simba and his brother became fully grown, their father chased them away. All young male lions are forced to find their own territories and prides once they are old enough to take care of themselves. Although they must leave their family, the two brothers will stay together for the rest of their lives. At three years of age, Simba and his brother left their pride and entered a territory that belonged to a pair of large males. These males were fierce, so the brothers did not challenge them. Instead, they traveled on. They finally settled on a patch of land that no other lions wanted. There was very little game to hunt. The brothers wandered in this poor territory for two years.

At night they could hear the roars of the stronger lions that lived in prides. A pride lion's loud and long roar proclaims his territory and warns off other lions. One time Simba and his brother tried to take over a pride territory by challenging a lone male, but they were unsuccessful.

A few months later the two lions tried to wrestle a large territory away from two aging lions. A fierce battle took place. This time, however, because the old lions were weak, the two young males won. Sometimes lions are killed in these fights, but in this case the older ones both escaped. Simba and his brother quickly claimed the territory and the pride of seven females as their own.

*Always on the lookout, Simba winces as he detects the scent of another lion in his territory.*

## Protecting the pride

The males in most prides are brothers. They spend many of their waking hours traveling along the edges of their territories, keeping out other males and protecting the pride from predators such as hyenas and leopards. This is no easy feat! Pride territories can be very large, and the males may be on patrol for several days without seeing a single member of their pride.

## Marking boundaries

Patrolling lions warn off other males in a number of peaceful ways. Roaring is one method. On a quiet night a lion's roar can be heard four miles (six kilometers) away. Local tradition says that when a lion roars, he is really saying, "Whose land is this? Mine! Mine! Mine!" Male lions that hear this roar get the message loud and clear and usually stay away.

*Pride lions spend much of their time on patrol.*

The lions mark their boundaries by squirting urine on bushes or clumps of grass. This leaves behind the distinctive scent of a male lion. The pungent odor warns wandering males to stay away. Another peaceful way of keeping strange lions out is simply by being visible. Most enemies run away when they see Simba coming. By constantly guarding their territory, Simba and his brother ensure the safety of the pride.

## Losing a territory

Lions seldom manage to keep their territories for more than a few years. Stronger rivals usually take them over in fierce battles. It is possible for a lion that has lost his pride to take over another one, but this rarely happens. Defeated males usually become nomads that wander along the fringes of other lions' territories, surviving to the best of their abilities until old age or accidents end their lives.

# Strong lion, strong cub

Male lions want to have a territory so they can belong to a pride. Lions rely on lionesses to hunt their food. They also breed with these pride females. Only the best lions are capable of holding territories and fathering future generations. The characteristics that allow Simba to rule the pride—his strength and courage—are passed on to his offspring. Because only strong lions have the opportunity to mate, the cubs end up being strong as well. This is nature's way of making sure that the species remains healthy.

## Starting again

When Simba and his brother took over the pride, the first thing they did was kill all the newborn cubs of the defeated lions. They ate some, and the females ate the others. A few became food for jackals and vultures. New pride males always kill the offspring of former pride males so they do not waste valuable time and energy looking after cubs that are not their own. Females with young cubs are not able to breed again until the cubs are about two years of age. Males do not know how long they will rule a pride, so they want to breed with the females as soon as possible. This makes it necessary for the new rulers of the pride to kill the cubs. The lionesses then become fertile right away. The lions never kill cubs except when they are taking over a new pride.

Human beings sometimes have difficulty understanding the behavior of animals. Some people do not like the fact that lions kill cubs, nor can they understand why lionesses do not protect their offspring from intruding males. Although their actions appear cruel, these animals are neither good nor bad; they are just acting according to their natural instincts.

*(opposite) In zoos lions may live to be over twenty years old, but on the African savannah only one tenth of the male lions reach old age.*

*(right) When a lion takes over a pride, he mates with the females. This pair ignores potential prey such as the buffalo in the background.*

*(below) Pride lions love to lie around and doze. Simba's pride consists of seven lionesses, Simba, his brother, and all their offspring.*

# Life in the pride

Today, as Simba approaches the pride, a female stands up and greets him. Like two giant house cats they rub faces and sniff each other. Other females and a few of his cubs also join in the greeting ceremony. Tails stuck straight up, the lions rub against Simba. Then they all flop down and go to sleep.

Of all the members of the cat family only lions live in prides. Tigers do not live in groups—neither do cheetahs, leopards, or any other cats. Some hunters such as hyenas, wild dogs, and wolves live in packs. Most types of dogs seem to prefer groups, but of all the cats, only the lion shares this close-knit social system.

These family groups may hold only a few animals or as many as fifty. One pride living in a marsh near Simba's territory has only one male, two adult females, and four half-grown cubs. Simba's pride totals twenty-three lions, consisting of the two brothers, seven adult females, and several cubs.

*(below) Just as house cats rub up against family members when they greet, so do lions.*

*The pride lionesses spot some distant prey. All the members of the pride share in what these hunters catch.*

## Benefits of living together

Many scientists have studied lions to discover why they live in prides. One benefit of living in a pride is that the food is shared by all. By hunting together, the pride lions can tackle prey that would be too large for an individual lion to kill. A large animal provides enough meat to feed the entire pride, even the poor hunters. Because some lionesses are better hunters than others, their skills benefit the whole pride. Pride life also helps ensure cub survival. When the males are away patrolling and the lionesses are out hunting, at least one adult lion always stays behind to mind all the pride's cubs.

## Problems with prides

Living in prides can create problems, too. If there are many members to feed, a lot of prey must be killed. Often there is not enough food, and some family members go hungry. The lionesses of Simba's pride usually hunt great herds of antelope and zebra. Every year these herds travel to faraway places, leaving Simba's territory empty. As soon as the large herds are gone, the pride only has small prey or the dangerous buffalo from which to choose. This leads to disaster because, without enough food, many members of the pride starve to death. When food is really scarce, lions live solitary lives, hunting and feeding by themselves.

# The heart of the pride

# One big female family

Simba and his brother are only two of a long line of ever-changing males in this pride's territory. In time these two lions will be chased off by stronger and younger males that, in turn, will suffer a similar fate. The lionesses, however, never leave the pride into which they are born. They are the heart of the pride. The seven females in this group are part of a long line of related lionesses. They will stay together their whole lives.

# Great hunters

Female lions are important to the pride because they are such skillful hunters. They usually work as a team. They crouch down in the grass and sneak up on their prey by crawling so low that their bellies brush the ground. As they approach their prey, they spread out. When the prey begins to run, the closest lioness attacks. She grabs the animal with her long, sharp claws and pulls it to the ground. The masterful hunter kills quickly and neatly by smothering her prey or by breaking the animal's neck.

*(opposite) During the heat of the day lionesses often relax in the shade with their cubs.*

# Fertile felines

Female lions become fertile when they have no cubs. This can happen at any time of year. Lionesses see their mates come and go. They care little which male mates with them or defends their territory, provided he is capable of doing so. They might also mate with a wandering male while the pride males are away checking boundaries. Should an unrelated female try to enter the pride's territory, however, the lionesses behave quite differently. They immediately rally together and chase the stranger away.

# Caring for cubs

A lioness also gives birth to cubs and feeds and raises them. After carrying the cubs inside her uterus for nearly four months, she is ready to give birth. She finds a private spot in some undergrowth because she prefers to be alone during the birth process. A lioness gives birth to a litter of up to five cubs. Together the lionesses of the pride care for the cubs until the offspring are several years old. Their sons eventually leave, but their daughters stay behind as permanent members of the pride.

*(below) This alert lioness spots prey nearby.*

# Cute and pampered

Covered with fluffy, spotted fur, newborn cubs are blind, toothless, and helpless. Because they are mammals, their mother must nurse them and care for them or they would die. Lionesses produce milk, which the cubs suck from the teats on their mothers' bellies. The lioness lies down and nurses on her side. Her milk provides all the nutrition baby lions need.

## Hiding the cubs

A lioness hides her cubs well because hyenas, leopards, and even other lions prey on these defenseless creatures. She keeps her babies away from the pride and constantly changes their location. She hides them first in one spot, and then in another. To move them, she carefully picks each one up in her mouth by the scruff of its neck. She always checks to make sure that she has not forgotten any cubs. By three weeks of age the cubs are able to walk, but they still stay wherever their mother puts them. When the mother returns from hunting, the cubs greet her with much meowing, rubbing, and excitement.

## Part of the family

When they are two months old, lion cubs are big enough to join the group and keep up with the other pride members. At first the cubs are a bit nervous of the other lions—especially the big males. The older cubs leap towards the new cubs because they want to play, but the newcomers are frightened. They run back to their mother for protection. They hide behind her and rub their faces vigorously against her cheeks for reassurance. Soon they feel brave enough to play with the other cubs in the pride and join in the routine of pride life.

## Play or school?

Just as kittens love to play, so do lion cubs. Waving grass, flying butterflies, and the black tufts at the end of swishing tails all spark the curiosity of cubs. Fascinated by the world around them, the cubs run and tumble, investigate and pounce. They wrestle with one another as well as with the adults. Much of this play is practice for the future. When a cub stalks a grasshopper, it is developing hunting skills. Many mammal mothers spend months teaching their offspring how to survive in the wilderness. When the cubs are a bit older, the lionesses gradually teach the youngsters hunting techniques.

## The feeding order

Although cubs continue nursing until they are seven months old, they also begin eating meat just a few months after birth. As long as there is plenty of food, the cubs have a good life. When there is not enough meat to go around, however, the cubs may go hungry. The pride males are bigger and stronger than the others,
so they eat first, even though the lionesses hunt the food. The cubs eat last. Sometimes the males take a bigger piece of meat than they can eat. This saves the cubs from going hungry because males sometimes share with the cubs or let them steal morsels of food.

## Maintaining the numbers

As skillful hunters as the lionesses are, they still lose half their cubs to starvation each year. Nature, though, has a way of ensuring that more cubs will be born very soon. If her cubs should die, a lioness would stop nursing, and her milk would dry up. She would then be ready to breed and become pregnant once again. If cubs die because of starvation, they are soon replaced by a new litter. Should a lioness die or be unable to nurse her cubs, one of the other females would allow them to nurse from her.

*(opposite) A cub hides in the grass while Mom hunts.*

*(below) By the time the cubs are about two weeks old, they can see the world through cloudy blue eyes. Afer a few months, the color changes to amber.*

# Lion facts

## Cleaning and preening

Pride lions spend a great deal of time cleaning and preening one another's fur. They continue licking even when the other cats are clean—just for the fun of it. Although mutual licking makes lions happy, they never purr in pleasure as house cats do. Lions hum instead!

## Lion language

Lions are famous for their frightening roars. The sound of roaring lions on a distant hilltop can send other animals scurrying to safety. But lions make many other sounds, too. They hum when they are happy, cough to warn someone off, and woof when they are startled. A deserted cub bleats mournfully, two greeting lions puff at each other, and an angry lion hisses or snarls. Cubs meow constantly, which helps their mothers keep track of them.

## Sensitive senses

Living in the wild is demanding, but the lion is equipped with excellent senses of smell and hearing. A lost lion can use its nose just as a hunting dog can. It simply puts its nose to the ground, finds a trail left by another pride member, and follows it home! Lions have such a keen sense of hearing that they wake up at the tiny bleat of a far-off gazelle.

## Greedy gluttons

In order to stay healthy, lions need to eat thirteen pounds (six kilograms) of meat a day. Lions, however, do not eat every day. Some hunts fail, and others succeed so well that the lions can eat to their hearts' content—and lions love to eat. They eat and eat, take a rest, and then return to eat again. The largest lions can eat as much as ninety pounds (forty kilograms) at one time! After gorging themselves, their stomachs wobble back and forth as they walk.

*Lions share food when there is plenty to go around.*

## The manly mane

The distinctive manes of male lions come in many shades. Some are silver-gray, others are dark brown or light brown with dark tips. Lions are very proud of their furry frames and constantly lick them to keep them fluffy. Manes make their heads look so big that male lions can be seen quite a distance away, thereby warning away other lions. If a lion gets into a fight, his thick mane helps protect his skin from being cut or slashed. His mane is also useful for attracting females. A lion struts back and forth in front of a lioness, showing off his handsome physique and fluffy hairdo, hoping she will be impressed.

*This lion is roaring. A roaring lion does not look like the yawning lion on the opposite page.*

## Seeing like a cat

Lions have sensitive eyes that are specially adapted for night vision. Lions can change the size of their pupils to let in more or less light. In the bright sunlight of day, the pupils contract to thin vertical slits to prevent too much light from getting in. In the darkness of night their pupils expand to huge black circles to let in as much light as possible. Lions cannot hunt in complete darkness, but they can see well when there is even a small amount of moonlight.

*Although lions are usually in excellent shape, they sleep about eighteen hours every day!*

## Lazy bullies?

Lions, both male and female, like to sleep a lot. On average, they rest between eighteen and twenty hours a day! People often think of male lions as being lazy bullies because they do not hunt. Male lions are not as good at hunting as females because they frighten off the prey with their huge manes. If they need to, however, they can bring down prey on their own.

## Killer-sharp claws

Lions keep their long claws sharpened to a dangerous point by raking them down the trunk of a nearby tree several times a day. As many as five cats claw at the same tree at once. When lions do not need their claws, they retract them and keep them tucked away until these sharp weapons are needed during a hunt.

## Tempting tails

Tails are handy appendages. Lions use them for balancing, flicking away flies, and saying hello. A lion's tail is long and thin, with a dark tuft of fur at the end. An angry lion swishes its tail rapidly back and forth. Lion cubs find this lively "prey" particularly fascinating and spend hours pouncing on it.

## Lion up a tree

Some lions never climb trees, but others do all the time. They climb up to get away from flies and other insects in the grass or to get out of the way of a herd of elephants or buffalo. Others avoid the heat of the day by dozing in the shady branches where cool breezes blow. Getting up a tree can be difficult for a lion with a full belly, but getting down can be dangerous. Some lions are so heavy, they fall on their heads!

## The king of beasts

Human beings have always been fascinated by the strength and grace of the majestic lion. This noble creature appears in many of our myths, legends, and fairy tales, inspiring awe and fear. We use the lion as a symbol on flags and family crests. Some famous people have even been named after lions. King Richard the Lion-Heart was admired for his lionlike courage.

*The lion is called the king of beasts, but the lioness does most of the hunting.*

# Life on the savannah

In the heat of the day Simba seeks the shade of a convenient tree and joins the rest of his pride for a communal snooze. The lions cuddle together while they sleep. Surrounded by the waving grass, Simba is soon fast asleep.

## The savannah ecosystem

Simba and his pride are part of the savannah ecosystem. An ecosystem is a community made up of living and non-living parts. The non-living parts include the soil, rocks, water, gases in the air, and energy from the sun. These parts make up the physical environment.

The creatures that belong to the living part of the ecosystem depend on one another and on the physical environment. The living community includes the vegetation of the area and the insects, birds, and animals that inhabit it. People, animals, and insects consume the plants that produce food energy. Some consumers are herbivores; others are carnivores. Herbivores eat plants, and carnivores eat other animals.

## Grass: the great producer

Grass is crucial to the savannah ecosystem because it is the main producer. It absorbs energy from the sun, which it uses to produce food energy. To the untrained eye all the grass on the plains looks similar. In fact, several kinds of grasses flourish there because the soil differs from place to place. Some grasses have stiff, woody stems, whereas others bend easily. Some have broad, tall leaves, and others are short and narrow. Each plant is suited to particular conditions. The various types of soil on the grassland are among the best in the world because they were formed from volcanic ash and are rich in nutrients.

*The lions in Simba's pride live in an area of the African savannah where acacia and thorn trees dot the landscape.*

# The green and yellow grassland

The grass surrounds Simba in every direction. During the rainy season the lush savannah looks like a paradise on earth. A glorious green grass covers the plain. A few gnarled acacia trees dot the landscape. Because the African savannah is far from large bodies of water, the area receives little precipitation for several months of the year. Trees need a lot of moisture to survive, but grasses can manage with much less water. Grass also needs a great deal of sunshine to grow, so grasslands thrive where trees do not. In the dry season the yellow grass appears dead. Grasses, however, have huge root systems that keep the plants alive below ground. Even when there is a fire, the roots remain unharmed. When the rains come, the grass shoots up, growing four inches (ten centimeters) in six days. Some grasses grow to seven feet (two meters) in height.

## The grazers

Immense herds of grazers, animals that eat only grass, thrive on the rich savannah. The antelope, zebra, and gazelle do not have to compete with one another because each eats different types or parts of the grass. For instance, zebra eat the rough tops of the grass, wildebeest eat the tender middle section, and the Thompson gazelle nibble at the nutritious leaf tips. Wart hogs dig out the roots and bulbs below ground. None of the grazers ever kills the grass. A few weeks after the grazers move to another area, the vegetation grows back.

## The predators

The savannah grasses, which feed the herbivores, also provide the predators with plenty of prey. Predators are carnivores that hunt and kill for food. Besides the lion, the cheetah, leopard, wild dog, and hyena are all savannah predators. They keep the population of the grazers under control. If there were too many herbivores, they would damage the grassland by overgrazing. Thus, these predators play an important role in maintaining the balance of the savannah ecosystem.

# Scavengers and decomposers

Some carnivores eat the remains of animals that die of natural causes or were left by predators. Scavengers such as the vulture and the jackal make sure no meat goes to waste. After this cleanup crew has picked a carcass clean, the insects get to work consuming the last bits of nourishment. Certain insects and bacteria help break down the remains. They are called decomposers. The decomposers return the nutrients to the earth so these substances can nourish the soil. It does not take long for every trace of a kill to vanish—even the bones. There is never waste in a well-balanced ecosystem.

*These moth larvae are eating the remains of a wildebeest skull. Soon there will be nothing left.*

# A teeming community

The savannah ecosystem maintains the delicate balance of nature. In the tall, yellow grass a life-and-death struggle constantly takes place. The grass provides a perfect home for a wide variety of insects, which are a source of nourishment for the small rodents, birds, and reptiles. Other rodents and hares feed on seeds and herbs. These small animals are eaten by jackals, foxes, snakes, and birds of prey such as owls, hawks, and falcons. These carnivores are, in turn, kept in check by the large carnivores of the plain. In this way energy is passed along a food chain. Many overlapping food chains form a food web. Food webs demonstrate how animals live in an interconnected community.

# The grassland grazers

The grassland of the savannah is dry for part of every year. The rainy season does not start until late summer. The rainfall brings the new grass, which attracts herds of zebra and wildebeest to the pride's territory. The herds stay for several months before they head for the southern plains.

## Great wildebeest herds

Some 250,000 common zebra and 80,000 buffalo graze the plains. Outnumbering all other grazers combined is the wildebeest, of which there are over one million. This dark, ungainly antelope is also known as a gnu. Great herds of thousands of wildebeest travel to Simba's part of the savannah in long lines that stretch on and on. Because the wildebeest is the lion's main source of food, late summer is the best hunting season for the lion.

## The watchful antelope

Many types of graceful antelope populate the plains. Like other members of the ox family, antelope have split hooves, making them surefooted animals. They are herbivores and have hollow horns. Most species of antelope originated in Africa. The wildebeest is the most numerous. Scattered about in small herds are the topi and the kongoni. They have long noses so they can feed on the bases of the tall grasses and still keep their eyes above the waving sea of grass. They live in herds of up to twenty animals. Topi often stand on termite mounds to keep an eye out for predators. The largest antelope, the eland, is the size of a horse. Lions love to hunt the eland because it makes a big meal, but this species is rare on the plains. The impala and the tiny dik-dik are browsers that feed on bushes and trees instead of grasses.

*(left) Zebra are a favorite prey of lions. They are large enough to feed an entire pride.*

*(below) Grant's gazelle are small, so lions only hunt them when large animals are scarce.*

## The delicate gazelle

The most graceful antelope is the gazelle. The savannah where Simba lives has between a quarter and a half million Thompson gazelle. Each Tommy, as it is sometimes called, has a black slash on both its sides and an ever-wagging tail. These tiny animals rarely weigh more than forty-five pounds (twenty kilograms). When times are good, pride lions do not bother hunting Tommies because they are not big enough to feed even one lion. A larger version of the Tommy is the Grant's gazelle. In bad times both types of gazelle keep lions from going hungry.

## The zebra

The many-striped zebra can be seen scattered among the great herds of wildebeest. The zebra, a member of the horse family, lives peacefully with the wildebeest. The two species alert each other to danger. Within the larger herd, zebra stay together in family groups composed of a stallion, several mares, and their foals.

*(right) Wildebeest, the most numerous antelope on the savannah, move in huge herds. Imagine the sound of a thousand wildebeest all grazing at once.*

*(below) Impala feed on leaves.*

## Staying alive

How do herbivores protect themselves against the predators of the savannah? They have no claws or sharp teeth, but some do have horns and hard hooves. These features, however, cannot ensure protection against a fierce lioness. Grazers stay alive by avoiding attacks. Every eye, ear, and nose in the herd is on the alert for dangerous predators. Many species have protruding eyes so they can see in many directions at once. If a predator starts coming towards a herd, the animals simply run away. Grazers also hide from predators by using camouflage. Most grazers on the plain have stripes or spots that help them blend in with their surroundings. The color-blind lion can only see distant animals when they move. Grazers also avoid being overhunted by having all their young at one time. In spring the wildebeest cows have their calves within a one-week period. Because there are so many babies, the predators cannot possibly catch every one.

# The predators

Besides the lion, a variety of predators live on the grassland. These carnivores compete with lions for the available prey. Some hunt in large groups or packs. Others are solitary hunters.

## The spotted leopard

In the forested areas near the rivers lives the leopard, an animal that always hunts alone. This spotted cat, half of Simba's weight, hunts by ambushing its prey. It jumps from the branches of trees or dashes out of the long grass when the prey wanders within range. A mother is seldom accompanied by her youngsters in the hunt. Unable to defend its prey against other meat-eaters, the leopard usually drags its kill into a tree for safekeeping.

Lions and leopards both hunt the antelope, so they are bitter enemies. As a rule lions do not hunt in the forested areas and therefore seldom come across leopards. If they should meet one, however, they make every attempt to kill it. Leopards do not like lions either. They kill and eat unprotected lion cubs.

## The cheetah

Another spotted cat is the cheetah—the fastest land animal in the world. Cheetahs prefer to hunt on the open plain, so they are more likely to meet a lion than leopards are. Lions and cheetahs do not get along either. Fortunately the cheetahs hunt in the heat of the day, when the lions are resting. Instead of stalking through the tall grasses, these fast cats rely on their great speed to catch their prey. The cheetah hunts alone by quickly dashing towards the chosen animal. It can run sixty-eight miles (110 kilometers) per hour. Yet, for all its speed, a cheetah fails more often than it succeeds. Like all cats, it has small lungs so it often tires out before catching its prey.

## Packs of dogs

Besides the lion only the hyena and the wild dog hunt in large groups. Of the three, the wild dog is the most cooperative in sharing its food. Packs of as many as fifty dogs live together quite peacefully. Every member of the pack takes part in caring for the pups. Besides drinking their mothers' milk, pups under ten weeks of age are fed meat. The adults gulp down huge chunks of meat, return to the young, and then regurgitate, or bring the food back up. Older pups are always brought to the kill and allowed to eat before the others begin.

## Successful hunters

The hunt begins when the dominant male or female dog strikes out onto the plains. This leader is soon followed by the others. They greet one another and then split off, heads lowered in the hunting position. Soon they spot their usual prey, a gazelle. They try to get as close to the gazelle as they can before starting the chase. The gazelle recognizes the hunting posture of the dogs and starts running long before it would if it had seen a lion or a cheetah. The gazelle has good reason for running. Unlike cats, wild dogs have huge lungs and can run for great distances. Lions succeed only three times out of every ten attempts at hunting. Dogs and hyenas succeed nearly six times out of ten!

## The hyena

The hyena is a ninety pound (forty-kilogram) animal that seems to be part cat and part dog. This spotted predator has a bushy black tail. Clans of up to one hundred of these social animals live together in large dens. They are not as cooperative in hunting as wild dogs are. The whoops of one hyena alerts the others to the chance of a successful kill. All the clan members then come running. Hyenas never share their food with one another. It is every hyena for itself! Many die in squabbles over food.

*(opposite, top) A cheetah glances up to check for scavengers as her cubs eat. Cheetahs always gulp down their meals quickly because they are not big enough to defend their kill.*

## Competing for food

Lions and hyenas are natural enemies. They are in direct competition because both hunt the same prey and live in the same habitat. In Simba's grassland both species number about five thousand individuals. Lions kill hyenas if they can catch them, but they never eat them. Hyenas are believed to kill more lion cubs than any other predator. They were once thought to be cowardly scavengers that fed on the kills of others, but the hyena is now known to be a deadly hunter—especially at night. Hyenas kill about two thirds of the food they eat. In fact, lions often steal the hyena's kill. Despite competition from the hyena, the lion remains the dominant hunter on the savannah.

## Natural ways of predators

Many people get upset when they see how the wild dog and hyena kill their victims. Both species begin to eat the prey before it has died. They open up the belly and feed while the helpless victim watches in shock. Lions and other cats kill by suffocation. They clamp their jaws over the throat or mouth of their prey until it is dead. Watching lions kill is not nearly as bothersome to humans as watching wild dogs kill. Human values should not be used to judge either animal, however. In the wild no animal is good or bad. Their ways of killing are natural.

*(below) A hyena steals a meal.*

# A lion hunt

Simba and the other dozing lions wake up to the sound of distant hooves. A mixed herd of zebra and wildebeest move nervously through the long grass. They are heading towards a water hole. Three of the lions poke their heads up and stare in the direction of the herd. The wildebeest have come so close that the lionesses decide to attempt a kill. This is unusual because lions prefer hunting at night under cover of darkness. Their keen eyesight allows them to hunt whenever there is moonlight.

The lions are hunting during the day because they are hungry. One by one they move towards the herd, spreading out as they go. They crouch down very low, hiding in the tall grass. Simba, his brother, the other females, and the cubs watch the three lionesses go. None bothers to follow. Perhaps they know that too many hunters might spoil the chance of success. Perhaps they are just too sleepy.

## Spotting the lioness

One of the zebra spots a lioness and brays, sounding the alarm. No one panics. All the animals in the herd stop and stare at the cat. A predator that has been seen is not as dangerous as one that goes unnoticed. The lioness knows that she has been spotted, so she stands up in full view as if a hunt were the farthest thing from her mind. Then she lies down, and, after a pause, the herd moves on. For the moment the grazers are safe.

*The lionesses sink lower into the grass as they wait for a herd to move closer.*

## Tricked by the wind

Following right behind the first group is a second herd, also consisting of wildebeest and zebra. As the herd moves closer, one lioness sneaks down to some bushes near a small river, and the other two crouch in the grass. It seems like a perfect ambush, but the wind, which is at their backs, blows straight towards the herd. The grazers smell the lions and, before the cats have a chance to attack, they move back over the hill. For all their hunting abilities lions have no idea that their scent is carried by the wind.

## Third-time lucky

An hour passes. The lionesses are joined by six half-grown cubs. They are positioned around the water hole when a third mixed herd comes into view. This time the wind is blowing from the herd towards the lions, so the grazers do not smell or see the lions. The zebra and wildebeest know that bushes and water holes are dangerous places where predators often hide. They pause and wait. For a few minutes they do nothing except stare and sniff the air. Then two zebra edge slowly towards the water.

The first lioness springs into action. The herd panics and bunches together, starting a stampede. The lioness singles out a wildebeest cow and races after it. The wildebeest crashes through some underbrush, which slows her down just enough for the lioness to catch up and hook her claws into a back leg. The terrified animal is sent sprawling in a cloud of dust and grass. Death quickly follows.

The other two females have also been successful in bringing down a wildebeest. Three cats, two kills—a remarkable feat. There will be enough food for the whole pride. As for the survivors in the herd, they turn away and continue their journey.

*The herd (top) stampedes when the lioness charges. The hunters (middle) follow in hot pursuit. After the kill, Simba (right) keeps the others away from his portion.*

# What a feast!

A lion kill benefits many more animals than just the hunter. As soon as the lionesses make their kills, a long chain of events is set into motion. First, the other lions in the pride gather at the kill site. Simba and his brother keep one animal for themselves and let the females and cubs squabble over the other. The adults tear open the carcasses with their sharp teeth and dig in. The abundance of meat allows every lion to eat to satisfaction. After the meal, the pride wanders down to the water hole for a drink and a snooze.

*A tawny eagle and a griffon vulture wait for three jackals to finish eating before it is their turn to pick at the leftovers.*

## The cleanup crew

Other animals quickly arrive to feast on the remains of the wildebeest. The vultures are the first to come. Vultures are huge birds that eat meat, but because they are scavengers, they never kill an animal themselves. On the savannah, vultures eat more meat than all other predators combined. With their excellent eyesight, they see the lions feasting and begin a slow descent. This signals other vultures that food is available, so they also come to share in the spoils.

Jackals are the next to arrive. There are hardly any vultures at the kill, so the jackals chase them away. One way or another most of the remains are stripped from the bones. The bones and horns are also useful. The hyenas crack open the strongest bones to feed on the soft inner portion called the marrow. Insects lay eggs in the remains of the horns and, when the young hatch, they feed on the remaining bits of nourishment.

## An after-dinner confrontation

Sometimes events on the plains take on a comic air. Such an event begins to unfold shortly after the lions arrive at the water hole. First a herd of buffalo comes lumbering over the hill, determined to get a drink. The sleepy lions are too full to bother hunting. It would be hard work because buffalo are large, aggressive creatures that will challenge anything that happens to cross their path. This time, however, the buffalo have too many newborns to risk a confrontation. They decide to go without a drink and continue on to the next water hole.

## Buffalo bullies

At dusk a smaller group of buffalo surprises the pride. A big bull with massive horns moves towards Simba. His head is lowered in an aggressive gesture. Simba stares at the huge, black animal. He knows that he is no match for the short-tempered bull. If lions attack a buffalo from behind, they are able to stay away from its dangerous horns. Attacking one from the front is another matter. When the bull finally works himself into a fury and charges, Simba and the lionesses run for their lives.

## A final retreat

An hour later a third buffalo herd comes to the water hole. The pride lionesses crouch and begin to stalk. This time several buffalo charge, scattering the cats. The lions look less than dignified after being chased up onto a narrow rock ledge for safety. Crowded on this ledge, they seem to be aware that they have been bullied!

*This angry buffalo charges towards Simba and the others, chasing them onto a rocky ledge. They wait until the coast is clear before moving on.*

# Poachers—the superpredators

On a ridge near the lion pride stand the last two black rhinoceros in the region. These magnificent animals have huge horns that are treasured by some cultures. At one time there were hundreds of thousands of black rhinos in Africa, but now fewer than ten thousand remain. Because rhinos are on the brink of extinction, they are considered an endangered species. Most of the rhinos in the world have been killed off by poachers, people who hunt animals illegally. Rhino poachers kill the animals to make money from the sale of the horns. Rhino horns are ground up as medicinal powder in the Far East or fashioned into dagger handles in the small country of Yemen. One horn sells for more than $10,000.

Poaching is a difficult problem in Africa because not all poachers are out to make money. The poachers who carry off rhino horns nearly always leave the meat behind to rot. Some poachers, however, kill wild animals because it is the only way they can feed their hungry families. Many people in Africa starve to death each year because there is not enough food for everyone. Can you blame a hungry father for killing one of the millions of grazers so he can feed his starving child? On the other hand, can you imagine the disaster if all the wild animals disappeared from earth? There are no easy answers.

***Black rhinos are disappearing because poachers kill them for their horns.***

## Lion poachers

Poachers have not left lions alone, either. At one time lions were shot as pests. Now African nations want to save their lions because they attract tourists who bring money into the country. But tourists like to take home souvenirs. Some people buy lion claws, tails, and heads. Local people make a living by poaching lions for their hides and, in some places, the lion populations have dropped noticeably. No one knows for sure how many lions are poached illegally each year. Lions have fared better than the black rhino because they can have more babies each year. Will lions, too, face extinction in the near future?

## Simba gets caught

Both Simba and his brother have nearly been killed by poachers. They were once caught in snares. Snares are traps made of thin wires that pull tightly around an animal's body. Death from such a device is slow and painful. It may take weeks for death to come as the wire cuts slowly into the flesh and infection sets into the wound. Simba and his brother would have died had park rangers not rescued them. The rangers removed the wires, treated the lions' wounds, and set the brothers free.

## Where have all the lions gone?

Lions have disappeared from North Africa and Arabia. A handful remains in India in a reserve called the Gir Forest. Only in Africa, in the savannah and the forested plains, do many lions still live in the wild, but farmlands and cities are growing quickly, and human progress is robbing the lion of its territories. Increasingly, lions can only find safety in national parks and game reserves.

*Simba's brother grew thin while caught in a poacher's snare. Can you see his wound? Rangers rescued him and treated his injuries.*

# This land is mine!

It is nearly dusk and the temperature on the African grassland is dropping rapidly. The night will be cool. A lioness stretches and stares out across the plain. In the distance she sees a mixed herd of wildebeest and zebra trekking away from a water hole. The noisy maaing and braying of these grazers mingles in the cool evening air. They are nervous because the lions and hyenas are most deadly at night.

Simba stirs, too, and yawns. He walks over to the lioness and then roars. His message is clear. "This land is mine," he says, his roar rolling across the reserve. When he stops, there is silence. The day is done, and the events of the night are about to unfold. Simba and the pride rouse themselves and slip quietly into the darkness. Their future, at least for now, is secure.

*(opposite) As the sun sets, a lioness heads out on the grasslands in search of prey.*

*(right) Simba's brother yawns before he heads out to patrol the territory.*

*(below) Simba contentedly gnaws on a piece of bone. As long as the African savannah is protected, Simba and other lions will be able to live as they please.*

# Glossary

**acacia** - A large flowering tree or shrub able to survive on the dry African savannah

**browser** - An animal that feeds on the leaves and shoots of bushes and trees

**camouflage** - The color or pattern of an animal or object that helps it blend in with its surroundings

**carnivore** - A meat-eating animal

**cub** - A baby of any member of the cat or bear family

**decomposer** - An organism such as a worm, fungus, or bacteria that reduces what it eats into nutrients, which are then returned to the environment

**ecosystem** - An interdependent community of plants and animals and the surroundings in which they live

**endangered** - Close to becoming extinct

**environment** - The surroundings in which an animal or plant lives

**extinct** - Describing species that no longer exist

**fertile** - Capable of producing offspring

**gazelle** - A small, delicate antelope of northern Africa that can run at high speeds

**grassland** - A plain on which grasses are the main form of vegetation

**grazer** - An animal that feeds on grasses

**habitat** - The area in which a plant or animal naturally lives

**herbivore** - A plant-eating animal

**herd** - A group of wild animals that wanders together. Zebra and wildebeest live in herds.

**litter** - A group of animals born to one mammal mother at the same time

**mammal** - An animal that is warm-blooded, covered in hair, and has a backbone. A female mammal has mammary glands that produce milk.

**mate** - The partner with which an animal breeds

**mating** - The act of coupling for the purpose of breeding

**nomad** - A person or animal that travels from place to place often in search of food or water

**nutrient** - A substance that a living thing consumes to be healthy and strong

**poacher** - A person who kills wild animals unlawfully

**predator** - An animal that hunts and kills other animals for food

**pride** - A small group of lions that lives together in a territory

**reserve** - An area set aside for animals to live in the wild

**savannah** - Any large area of tropical or subtropical grassland covered, in part, by trees and spiny shrubs

**scavenger** - An animal that feeds on the remains of animals that it did not hunt and kill

**species** - A distinct animal or plant group that shares similar characteristics and can produce offspring within its group

**territory** - An area of land an animal claims as its own

**uterus** - The organ of a female mammal in which the young develop and are protected before birth

# Index

Africa  5, 19, 20, 28, 29, 30
antelope  11, 19, 20, 21, 22
birth  13
black rhinoceros  28
browsers  20
buffalo  9, 11, 17, 20, 27
camouflage  21
cheetahs  10, 19, 22, 23
claws  13, 17, 25, 29
cleaning  16
cubs  8, 10, 11, 12, 13, **14-15**, 16, 22, 23, 25
ecosystems  **18-19**
eyes  15, 17, 24
food  11, 15, 16, 23, 25, **26-27**
fur  14, 16
gazelle  16, 19, 20, 21, 23
grasslands  (see savannah)

grazers  19, 20, 21, 24, 25, 28
hearing  16
hunting  5, 8, 11, 13, 14, 15, 16, 22, 23, **24-25**, 26
hyenas  7, 10, 14, 19, 23, 26, 30
impala  20, 21
insects  19, 26
jackals  8, 19, 26
leopards  7, 10, 14, 19, 22
lionesses  8, 11, **12-13**, 14, 15, 24, 25, 26, 27, 30
mammals  14, 15
manes  5, 16
nursing  14, 15, 23
patrolling  5, 6, 11, 31
poaching  **28-29**
predators  7, 19, 20, 21, **22-23**, 24, 26, 28

prey  11, 13, 19, 22, 23
prides  5, **6-13**
reproduction  **8-9**, 13
reserves  5, 30
roaring  6, 7, 16, 30
savannah  5, 9, **18-23**, 30, 31
scavengers  19, 23, 26
senses  16
sleeping  9, 10, 17, 18, 26, 27
tails  17, 29
territories  6, 7, 8, 10, 11, 13, 20, 31
vultures  8, 19, 26
wild dogs  10, 19, 23
wildebeest  5, 19, **20-21**, 24, 25, 26, 30
Yemen  28
zebra  5, 11, 19, **20-21**, 24, 25, 30

3 4 5 6 7 8 9  WP Printed in the U.S.A.  9 8 7 6 5 4 3